Canadian representatives: General Publishing Co., Ltd.,
30 Lesmill Road, Don Mills, Ontario M3B 2T6.

9 8 7 6 5 4 3 2 1
Digit on the right indicates the number of this printing.

ISBN 1–56138–363–5

Cover design by E. June Roberts
Interior design by Paul Kepple
Cover illustration by Kathy Lengyel
Interior illustrations by Paul Hoffman
Edited by Elizabeth Pokempner
Typography: Bodoni Book with Cochin and
Caslon OpenFace by Deborah Lugar

This book may be ordered by mail from the publisher.
Please add $2.50 for postage and handling.
But try your bookstore first!

Running Press Book Publishers
125 South Twenty-second Street
Philadelphia, Pennsylvania 19103–4399

GRANDMOTHER

a personal journal, with illustrations and quotations

running press • philadelphia, pennsylvania

Grandmothers don't have to do anything except be there. . . .

Patsy Gray
20th-century American child

We always believe those who resemble us.

Jean de la Fontaine (1621–1695)
French writer

Holding these babies in my arms makes me realize the miracle my husband and I began.

Betty Ford, b. 1918
Former American First Lady

First thing I do every day is look up at the moon. . . . I just go look at the moon to see how it is.

Lena Sooktis
20th-century Cheyenne Indian

I love clipping small pieces of plants and making them grow into big things.

Marian Wright Edelman, b. 1939
American activist and writer

I hang out with a lot of grandmas. Their grandchildren were all born in mangers and have IQs so high they cannot be measured. All of them vow that if grandchildren hadn't been invented, we'd have to import them from Japan.

Erma Bombeck, b. 1927
American writer

You know, I think I was really meant to be a grandmother. It was mothering that confused me all of those years.

Lois Wyse, b. 1926
American writer

. . . some of the things which seemed crucial and of earth-shaking importance when you were rearing your children have had the chaff sifted out of them by the years and you recognize that they are of minor, even trivial, size.

Celestine Sibley, b. 1917
American writer

If your baby is "beautiful and perfect, never cries or fusses, sleeps on schedule and burps on demand, an angel all the time" . . . you're the grandma.

Teresa Bloomingdale, b. 1930
American writer

Once the children were in the house the air became more vivid and more heated; every object in the house grew more alive.

Mary Gordon, b. 1949
American writer

Who turned on the lights? You did, by waking up: you flipped the switch, started up the wind machine, kicked on the flywheel that spins the years.

Annie Dillard, b. 1945
American writer

I don't pretend to be an ordinary housewife.

Elizabeth Taylor, b. 1932
American actress

[Grandma] would be among the first to express pride at your accomplishments, but she loved us enough to set us straight when we slipped up.

Marcy Demaree
20th-century American writer

She looked at me. She was seeing the years and days I had no way
of knowing, and she didn't believe me . . . yet a look came on her
face. It was the look of mothers drinking sweetness from their
children's eyes. It was tenderness.

Louise Erdrich, b. 1954
American writer

We danced on and on, unequal partners who in those moments absolutely loved all the inequalities about us, the jokiness, the seriousness. My grandmother was singing: her voice was loud and clear. She spun me for a long time. Our heads thrown back, legs stepping, arms pumping, our fingers intertwined.

Marcie Hershman
20th-century American writer

I didn't expect this child to be such a source of affection. He doesn't give his grandmother one kiss, or even two kisses. Instead, his kisses are a rainforest where the rain never stops falling, little soft kisses in whichever bit of my face is nearest at that moment.

Nell Dunn, b. 1936
English writer

When a child is born, so are grandmothers.

Judith Levy
20th-century American writer and editor

As I grew up . . . what was impenetrable to me was . . . mother's love for her own mother. Between these two there was no generation gap, no chasm. My mother never racked her brains explaining why she and her mother couldn't relate. Lavisa McElroy Loyd was Mama, and all her children felt the same fierce love for her.

Shirley Abbott, b. 1934
American writer

I would like them to be the happy end of my story.

Margaret Atwood, b. 1939
Canadian writer

I am an onlooker on my daughter's dance . . . I'm not part of her dance. Yet whenever she takes a pause and needs someone to talk to, I am there. But that special dance with the child and the future is hers.

Liv Ullmann, b. 1939
Norwegian actress and writer

It is as grandmothers that our mothers come into the fullness of their grace. When a man's mother holds his child in her gladdened arms, he is aware of the roundness of life's cycle; of the mystic harmony of life's ways.

Christopher Morley (1890–1957)
American writer

. . . there will be flowers in this landscape that do not grow
elsewhere, and glimpses of unforeseen heights.

Elizabeth Vining, b. 1902
American writer

Eternity is not something that begins after you are dead. It is going on all the time. We are in it now.

Charlotte Perkins Gilman (1860–1935)
American writer

I believe one thing, that today is yesterday and tomorrow is today and you can't stop.

Martha Graham (1884–1990)

American dancer

When you look at your life, the greatest happinesses are family happinesses.

Dr. Joyce Brothers, b. 1928
American psychologist

$$\text{W}\text{e are tomorrow's past.}$$

Mary Webb (1881–1927)
English writer

Heredity is an absorbing study—our forbears live in us and bear their part in all we do. This gives me a fresh zest for living when I look at my own grandchildren and see the thrill of life which was, in that older generation, reflected in them.

Sybil Thorndike Casson (1882–1976)
English actress

. . . seeing a child as one's grandchild, one can visualize that same
child as a grandparent, and with the eyes of another generation one
can see other children . . . who must be taken into account—now.

Margaret Mead (1901–1978)
American anthropologist

Family faces are magic mirrors. Looking at people who belong to us, we see the past, present and future.

Gail Lumet Buckley, b. 1937
American writer

Nature gives you the face you have at twenty; it is up to you to merit the face you have at fifty.

Coco Chanel (1883–1970)
French fashion designer

What could be more beautiful than a dear old lady growing wise with age?

Brigitte Bardot, b. 1934
French actress

In the Indian's thinking, the earth is the mother and the sun's the father, and we have all our relatives in the stars in between. . . .

Vickie Downey
20th-century Tewa Indian

Grandma ain't quite five feet tall, not much more'n me and Candy and we eight—or almost—years old. But Grandma's voice got ten feet of do-what-I-say in it, and the boys throw their gunsticks down quicker'n they be red hot coals.

Birthalene Miller
20th-century American writer

The older one grows, the more one likes indecency.

Virginia Woolf (1882–1941)
English writer

I have bursts of being a lady, but it doesn't last long.

Shelley Winters, b. 1922
American actress

I'm not as nice as you think I am.

The Queen Mother, b. 1900
English royalty

If you close your eyes just for a split second, you can sort of imagine your grandmother made those Pepperidge Farm "Down Home Style Donuts," even though your grandmother is presently a cocktail waitress in Atlantic City.

Stephanie Brush
20th-century American writer

She'd had her fortune told, her palm read, from time to time, the tarot. It was a comfort and she wasn't going to stop it. Not for a bunch of uppity know-it-alls. Gram sometimes seemed like the child of her daughters, the bad and willful one they couldn't do a thing with but loved the best because of her charm and daring.

Joan Chase
20th-century American writer

I don't brood about age myself. I just keep on changing.

Betty Friedan, b. 1921
American activist and writer

The true accolade was not only my father saying he would be proud of me, but that my grandmother would have been proud of me.

William H. Hastie (1904–1976)
American judge

Every time I think that I'm getting old, and gradually going to the grave, something else happens.

Lillian Carter, b. 1898
Mother of former U.S. President Jimmy Carter

If in fact your body may be slowing down, a different energy goes into self-reflection now, a deeper understanding of what you have lived; there's a gathering of all the parts, to knit them together consciously.

Suzanne Wagner
20th-century American psychoanalyst

Accept the pain, cherish the joy, resolve the regrets; then can come the best of benedictions—"If I had my life to do over, I'd do it all the same."

Joan McIntosh, b. 1943
American writer

The child in the old person is a precious part of his being able to handle the slow imprisonment. As he is able to do less, he enjoys everything in the present, with a childlike enjoyment. It is a saving grace. . . .

May Sarton (1912–1985)
Belgian-born American writer

I appreciate very much being alone now. In fact, I plan it. I hoard moments of being by myself and kind of charging my batteries. I think that you are more aware that as you get older you have to charge them a bit, deliberately, instead of just continuing on unlimited electrical energy.

M. F. K. Fisher (1908–1992)
American writer

The wrinkles aren't exactly pretty but they are—well, dear. . . .
If I managed to eradicate them . . . would my face be
as unmistakably mine?

Susan Jacoby
20th-century American writer

If you don't have wrinkles, you haven't laughed enough.

Phyllis Diller, b. 1917
American comedian

Adventure is something you seek for pleasure, or even for profit, like a gold rush or invading a country; . . . but experience is what really happens to you in the long run; the truth finally overtakes you.

Katherine Anne Porter (1890–1980)
American writer

Long after I have forgotten all my human loves, I shall still remember the smell of a gooseberry leaf, or the feel of wet grass on my bare feet. In the long run, it is this feeling that makes life worth living. . . .

Gwen Raverat
19th-century American writer

My kitchen linoleum floor is so black and shiny that I waltz while I wait for the kettle to boil.

Florida Scott-Maxwell (1883–1978)
Scottish-born American actress and writer

When one is too old for love, one finds great comfort in good dinners.

Zora Neale Hurston (1903–1960)
American writer

If God had intended us to follow recipes, He wouldn't have given us grandmothers.

Linda Henley, b. 1951
American writer

With both my children and my grandchildren I have encouraged them to reach high—not to think about what somebody else is doing but about what should be done. And I have always told them that the way to do it is to start with yourself first. And then just spread out.

Wendy Watriss
20th-century American writer

There is so much to teach, and the time goes so fast.

Erma Bombeck, b. 1927
American writer

Because time has been good to me, I treat it with respect.

Lena Horne, b. 1917
American vocalist

. . . my mother and I are still at cross purposes. Particularly since my daughters were born, she has whispered in my ear each night as I slept, trying to remake me in her image. I battle her off as well as I can, but she touches me still, and I love her. I would not want my children to grow up without knowing what their grandmother thought.

Shirley Abbott, b. 1900
American writer

My mother had no dreams to lay on my children. She had tried . . . and succeeded . . . and failed with my sister and me. She was done with that now and her grandsons couldn't defeat her. Or disappoint her. Or prove anything—anything good or bad—about her. And I saw her free of ambition, free of the need to control, free of anxiety. Free, as she liked to put it—to enjoy.

Judith Viorst, b. 1931
American writer

Grandparenthood is actually as much a complex state of being as adolescence or middle age.

Edwina Sherudi
20th-century American writer

I began to have an idea of my life, not as the slow shaping of achievement to fit my preconceived purposes, but as the gradual discovery and growth of a purpose which I did not know.

Joanna Field, b. 1900
English psychologist

I love my family for many reasons; for what I see them to be, for the loveliness that they have been, for the good I know in them. I love their essence, their "could be," and all this in spite of knowing their faults well. . . .

Florida Scott-Maxwell (1883–1978)
Scottish-born American actress and writer

How can we explain the places we finally land, after inexplicable journeys, long boring holidays, years of misapprehension? How do we finally find them—or do they find us, like a happening coming after a dream, which follows the dream's speech and action so that we say that it is our "dream out?"

Louise Bogan (1897–1970)
American poet and critic

Life is like a butterfly—you can chase it, or let it come to you.

Ruth Brown
20th-century American writer

A family is a river; some of it has passed on and more is to come, and nothing is still, because we all move along, day by day, toward our destination.

Dolores Garcia
20th-century Chicano grandmother

This is a circular book. It does not begin at the beginning and go on to the end; it is all going on at the same time, sticking out like the spokes of a wheel from the hub, which is me. So it does not matter which chapter is read first or last.

Gwen Raverat
19th-century American writer

As I've gotten older, I've gotten more sure of myself. I was a shy and withdrawn young mother; and I am not a shy and withdrawn grandmother.

Berniece Rooke
20th-century American grandmother

The things that I have instilled in my sons or grandsons or other people around me will live forever. That is me. . . .

Cecilia Mitchell
20th-century Mohawk medicine woman